PASTA

Kate Haycock

Illustrations by John Yates

Carolrhoda Books, Inc./Minneapolis

All words that appear in **bold** are
explained in the glossary on page 30.

First published in the U.S. in 1991 by
Carolrhoda Books, Inc.

Copyright © 1990 Wayland (Publishers) Ltd.,
Hove, East Sussex. First published 1990 by
Wayland (Publishers) Ltd.

Library of Congress Cataloging-in-Publication Data

Haycock, Kate.
    Pasta / Kate Haycock ; illustrations by John Yates.
        p.   cm. — (Foods we eat)
    Summary: Discusses the role of pasta in history and describes how
it is processed and prepared for meals. Includes recipes.
    ISBN 0-87614-656-6
    1. Pasta products—Juvenile literature. 2. Cookery (Pasta)—
Juvenile literature. [1. Pasta products.] I. Yates, John, 1939-
ill. II. Title. III. Series: Foods we eat (Minneapolis, Minn.)
    TX394.5.H38   1990
    641.8'22—dc20   90-46423
    HAY   CIP
                                                                                  AC

Printed in Italy by G. Canale & C.S.p.A., Turin
Bound in the United States of America

1 2 3 4 5 6 7 8 9 10 00 99 98 97 96 95 94 93 92 91

Contents

What is pasta?

Pasta is a type of food that is eaten all over the world. There are hundreds of different types of pasta. You've probably eaten pasta such as spaghetti, macaroni, and ravioli.

Pasta is a popular food because it is inexpensive, tasty, filling, and easy to prepare. It is also a healthy food. Pasta comes in many different shapes, types, and colors and can be prepared in many delicious ways.

People have been eating pasta for centuries. In the past, some people thought of pasta as a food eaten only by the poor, but now it is popular in many homes and fashionable restaurants.

Pasta in history

Pasta may have been brought to Italy by the explorer and merchant Marco Polo, seen here on his travels nearly 700 years ago.

Pasta is an Italian word meaning paste or dough. Pasta is made from dough that is rolled out and formed into different shapes. Italy is one of the places where people eat a lot of pasta. In Italy, people sometimes eat pasta at two meals a day.

Some people believe that pasta first came from

the island of Sicily, off the southern coast of Italy. Others claim that pasta was brought to Italy from China by Marco Polo. Marco Polo was an Italian merchant and explorer who traveled to China in 1295.

It is possible that pasta originally came from Asia. It has been a part of the Oriental diet for hundreds and perhaps thousands of years. Noodles are popular in Japanese, Chinese, and other types of Oriental cooking.

Pasta is an important part of the Oriental diet. Here, a chef is making pasta noodles in a Hong Kong restaurant.

7

Pasta as food

In recent years, many doctors and health experts have encouraged people to eat more pasta. Pasta is rich in **carbohydrates**, substances that help give us the energy we need to move, to walk, to run, and to play.

We can get carbohydrates from sugary foods, but the carbohydrates in pasta are much healthier for

Whole wheat pasta, like the spaghetti below, is a healthy food. It contains fiber as well as carbohydrates.

carbohydrates
protein
water
fat
vitamins and
minerals

Left: The nutritional value of pasta

Below: This pasta, stuffed with spinach and cheese, is popular with many vegetarians.

us. The energy we get from pasta lasts longer than energy from sugar. Athletes may eat a large bowl of pasta before a race or competition to give them more energy.

Pasta is also low in fat, which is a substance doctors say we should eat less of. Eating too many fatty foods can make us overweight and unhealthy. Some pasta, such as **whole wheat** pasta, is high in **fiber**, which is good for our digestive systems. Pasta can be served with vegetables or meatless sauces. For that reason, it is very popular with **vegetarians**.

Types of pasta

Pasta comes in many shapes and sizes. Here are two examples.

All pasta is cooked in boiling water and is usually served with a sauce to make a meal or side dish. The pasta that you buy at the supermarket is usually dried pasta.

You can buy pasta in many shapes and different colors. You've probably eaten the yellow spaghetti and macaroni that are sold in most stores, but have you ever had green pasta, which is made with spinach? What about brown **soba noodles** from Japan?

Some pasta is made with different fillings. Ravioli and tortellini, for example, are usually stuffed with meat or cheese. Other noodles and small pasta shapes are used in soups, such as chicken noodle and minestrone, or pasta salads.

Pasta is also available in cans, cooked in a cheese or meat sauce. Canned spaghetti and ravioli are popular with many children.

Fresh pasta, which takes less time to cook than dried pasta, is also sold in some stores. You can even make your own homemade pasta. It takes a long time to prepare, but many people think that homemade pasta is the most delicious pasta of all.

Above: Ravioli can be stuffed with spiced meat or with a cheese mixture.

Left: This pasta shop in Venice, Italy, displays some of the more unusual colors of pasta that you can buy.

11

What is pasta made from?

Pasta is made from simple ingredients, usually just flour and water. The flour comes from **durum wheat**, a type of hard-grained wheat that is grown mainly to be used in pasta making. Much of the durum wheat used in the United States is grown in North Dakota, South Dakota, Montana,

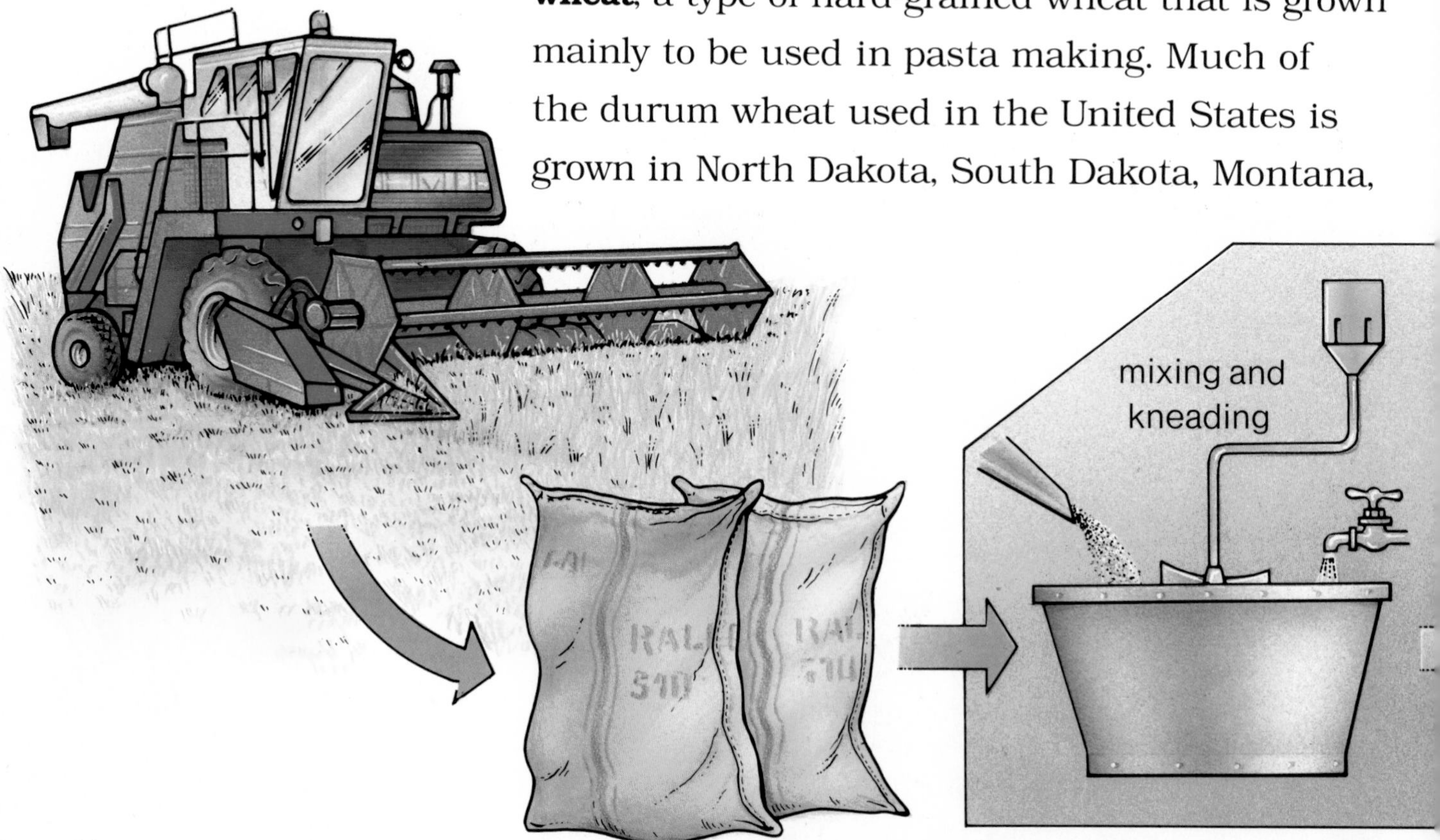

durum wheat harvested

mixing and kneading

and Minnesota.

Durum wheat is ground into **semolina**, a rough flour that is mixed with water to make a dough. The dough is forced through holes in metal plates or cut into the desired shapes, then dried.

In parts of Asia, a variety of different ingredients are used to make pasta. In addition to durum wheat, noodles are made from **buckwheat**, rice, beans, and even seaweed.

This diagram shows the different stages of pasta making in a factory.

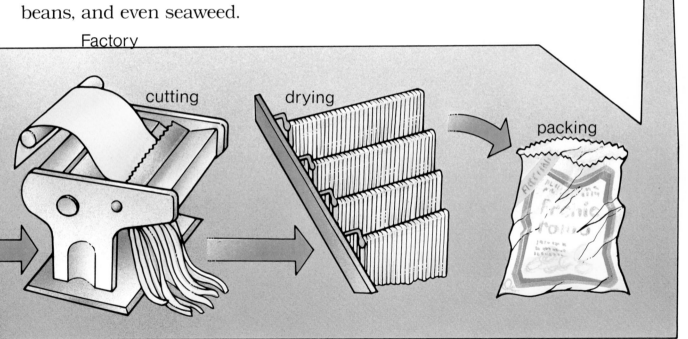

Factory

cutting

drying

packing

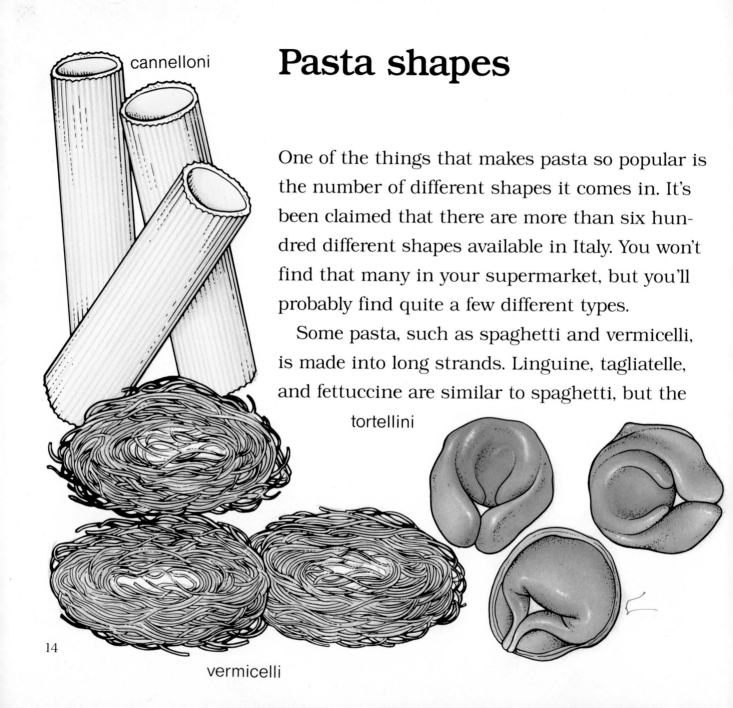

cannelloni

Pasta shapes

One of the things that makes pasta so popular is the number of different shapes it comes in. It's been claimed that there are more than six hundred different shapes available in Italy. You won't find that many in your supermarket, but you'll probably find quite a few different types.

Some pasta, such as spaghetti and vermicelli, is made into long strands. Linguine, tagliatelle, and fettuccine are similar to spaghetti, but the

tortellini

vermicelli

strands are flat.

Other pasta is rolled into tubes, like macaroni, cannelloni, and penne, or flat sheets, like lasagna. Some pasta, such as ravioli, is stuffed. Twists called fusilli are often used in pasta salads.

There are many other pasta shapes. Have you ever eaten bowties, shells, or wagon wheels made of pasta? Maybe you've had noodles shaped like letters of the alphabet or numbers. What other different pasta shapes can you find in the kitchen cabinet at home or on the shelves of your local supermarket?

Above: Try making a pasta picture like this one.

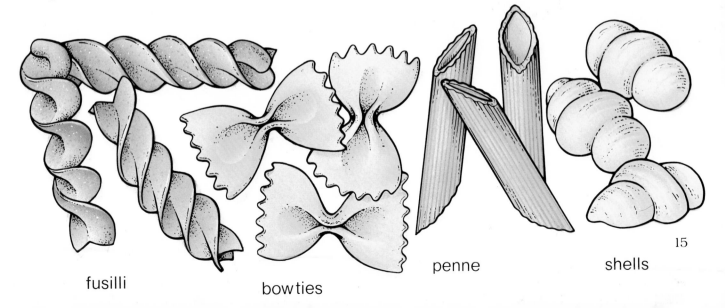

fusilli

bowties

penne

shells

Pasta around the world

Pasta is an important part of the Italian diet. This shop in Milan sells nothing but fresh pasta.

Many Italians eat pasta almost every day. At dinner, pasta is usually served as the second course. The first course is called the **antipasto**, which means "before the meal." A small portion of pasta is served between the antipasto and the main course. Pasta can also be eaten as the main part

Many foods, including pasta, are served at this Italian wedding feast.

of a light meal.

Many regions of Italy have favorite pasta dishes. For example, spaghetti Bolognese, served with a tomato, beef, and bacon sauce, is a specialty of the city of Bologna.

Noodles are a favorite food in Japan, China, and other Asian countries. Noodles are often served with meat or fish in broth or offered as a side dish instead of rice.

Making your own pasta

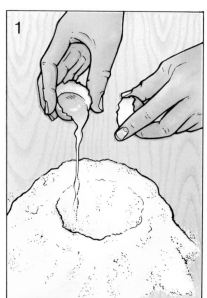

In Italian households, pasta was traditionally homemade. Homemade pasta is delicious, and although it can be difficult to make, it is fun to try. Ask an adult to help you.

You will need:

1 egg
1 cup of unbleached flour

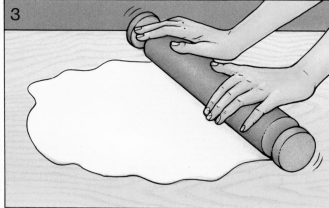

1. Put the flour on a large pastry board and make a well, or hollow, in the center. Break the egg into the well.

2. Knead the dough with your hands. Add some water if necessary.

3. Wrap the pasta dough in a damp cloth. Leave in the refrigerator for 15 minutes.

4. Roll out the dough very thin. Cut out the dough into the shapes you want.

Boil as for dried pasta, but only allow about 1-2 minutes cooking time.

This is a machine for making homemade pasta. Here, it is cutting pasta sheets into tagliatelle.

How to cook pasta

Pasta is very easy to cook if you remember to follow certain rules. First, make sure you use plenty of water, to allow the pasta room to move around during boiling. Do not leave the kitchen for a long period of time while the pasta is cooking. There is a saying in Italian that means "spaghetti loves

There are a wide variety of dishes that can be made with pasta, including Italian dishes such as lasagna, spaghetti Bolognese, and seafood linguine.

company"—so make sure you don't leave it on its own!

The difficult part is knowing when the pasta is ready. Many Italians like pasta **al dente**, which is cooked but still chewy. Overcooked pasta is soggy and too soft, while undercooked pasta is hard to eat. It may take practice before you learn to cook pasta that is just right.

This chef is laying out pasta sheets to dry in front of an open fire before cutting the pasta and cooking it.

Cooking dried pasta

1.   Take a large saucepan and fill it about three-quarters full with water. With the help of an adult, bring the water to a boil, and then add a little salt if desired.

2.   Carefully add the pasta to the boiling water. Stir to separate. Cover the saucepan so the water boils again. When the water is boiling, remove the lid and adjust the heat until the water is bubbling briskly.

3.   Dried pasta should take about 10-12 minutes to cook, so watch the clock. After about 10 minutes,

Slowly add the pasta to a saucepan of boiling water. These children are cooking pasta with the help of an adult. Always make sure there is an adult with you when you cook.

Left: Is the pasta ready yet? Test the pasta by letting a piece cool, then taking a bite.

Below: Be sure to drain off all the water, or the pasta will become soggy.

take a little bit out of the pan with a fork, wait for it to cool, and taste it. If it is still hard, it needs to cook longer. Check the pasta again every 1 to 2 minutes until it's done.

4. When you think it is ready, turn off the heat and remove the pan from the stove. Drain the pasta into a colander. Make sure to drain off all the water or the pasta will be soggy.

The pasta is now ready to serve with your favorite sauce (see recipes).

How to eat spaghetti

Pasta is eaten all over the world. These people are using chopsticks to eat noodles in Beijing, China.

Spaghetti is a long, thin type of pasta that a lot of people find difficult to eat. The easiest way to eat spaghetti is to cut it into shorter pieces with a knife, but you might want to try the "proper" way.

Left: Twirl a small amount of spaghetti onto your fork with the help of a spoon.

Below: When you've got a mouthful on your fork, pop it into your mouth.

Take your fork and put the prongs down into the spaghetti. Now turn the fork around and around so that the spaghetti winds around it. When there is enough for a mouthful twirled around your fork, put it into your mouth. Some people lean the fork against a spoon while they are winding the spaghetti.

Some people don't care what they look like when they are eating spaghetti—they just scoop a pile of it into their mouths!

Spaghetti Bolognese

You will need:

1 tablespoon oil
3 tablespoons chopped bacon
1 chopped onion
1 chopped carrot
1 chopped celery stalk
½ pound ground beef
1½ tablespoons tomato puree
1 cup beef stock or water
salt and pepper
12 ounces spaghetti

2. Add the beef and stir until browned evenly. Add tomato puree, beef stock, salt, and pepper. Simmer for 30 to 40 minutes.

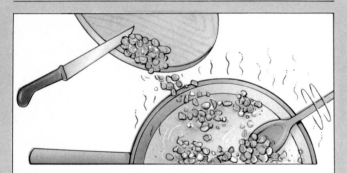

1. Heat the oil and cook the bacon, onion, carrot, and celery until the bacon is brown.

3. Boil the water for the spaghetti and cook according to the instructions on the package.

Fettuccine with mushrooms and cream

You will need:

6 ounces spinach fettuccine
2 tablespoons butter
2½ cups sliced mushrooms
1 teaspoon dried oregano
salt and pepper
4 tablespoons heavy cream

2. In a frying pan, melt the butter and add the mushrooms, oregano, salt, and pepper. Cover and cook for about 5 minutes.

1. Cook the pasta in a saucepan of boiling water.

3. When the pasta is ready, serve it with the sauce. Add a spoonful of cream over each serving. Add more pepper if you like.

Vegetarian lo mein

You will need:

8 ounces egg noodles
2 tablespoons oil
1 small onion, sliced
2 cups mushrooms, sliced
2 celery stalks, sliced
4 ounces bean sprouts
3 tablespoons soy sauce
3 tablespoons vegetable stock
1 teaspoon sugar

1. Cook the noodles in boiling water for 4 to 5 minutes.

2. Heat the oil in a frying pan and add the onion, mushrooms, and celery. Fry over high heat for 5 minutes, stirring often.

3. Drain the noodles and add them to the pan. Cook for another minute.

4. Add the bean sprouts, soy sauce, vegetable stock, and sugar. Cook for another 2 minutes, stirring well.

Glossary

al dente: cooked but still chewy, the preferred texture for cooked pasta. In Italian, *al dente* means "to the tooth."

antipasto: the first course of a traditional Italian meal. *Antipasto* means "before the meal" in Italian.

buckwheat: a type of edible grain that comes from the buckwheat plant

carbohydrates: substances in some foods that are an important source of energy

durum wheat: a hard-grained type of wheat that is grown mainly to be used in making pasta

fiber: the coarse, bulky material in some foods that helps keep our digestive systems healthy

semolina: a rough flour made from ground durum wheat

soba noodles: noodles made from buckwheat. Soba noodles are popular in Japan and other Oriental countries.

vegetarians: people who do not eat meat

whole wheat: food made from whole grains of wheat, including the outer covering or husk of the grain

Index

Photo acknowledgments

The photographs in this book were provided by: p. 6, Ronald Sheridan; pp. 7, 24, Hutchison Library; pp. 8, 9, 10, 11, 15, 17, 21, Anthony Blake Photo Library; pp. 16, 19, Topham Picture Library; p. 20, Bruce Coleman; pp. 22, 23 (both), 25 (both), Zul Mukhida.